Brown Sugar, Black Coffee

Khalil Ali

King and Queen Publishing, LLC

All Rights Reserved. No part of this publication may be used either in print or electronic form without the written consent of King and Queen Publishing, LLC. Published in the United States by King and Queen Publishing, LLC.

Copyright © 2016 by Khalil Ali

Cover illustration by Queen LaZae Ali

ISBN 978-0-9974226-0-3

For more information regarding personal appearances, interviews or purchases please contact the publisher at:

King and Queen Publishing, LLC

www.kingandqueenpublish.com

contact@kingandqueenpublish.com

To the woman that means all the world to me. You are my friend, my confidant, my love and my wife

This entire book and everything that it took for me to do this is for you.

Table of Contents

Adam & Eve 1

I Vow 5

I Say Yes 7

Anniversary 9

Appreciation 11

Away We Go 13

Be 15

Breath 16

Change Up 18

Crazy 21

Forever Will 23

Have Not 25

How Long? 27

Life Plus 20 29

Lose Control 31

Loving to Live 33

Moment in Time 35

Rainbow 37

Rainbows 39

RD 41

Shallow Words 43

Sit and Wonder 45

Symbol 46
Thinking/Reminisce 48
This Becomes That... 50
Tonight 52
Touch the Sky 53
Transitional Moments 55
Wait 57
Circles 59
Take One 61
Penny For Your Thoughts... 63

Adam & Eve

In the beginning when man was incompletely complete

Man was given woman to help him stay steady on his feet

This union of the mind, body and soul was perfectly excellent

3 parts in 1 flesh united with another became magnificent

There wasn't any need to interject the terrestrial with something that was way beyond human grasp

This was more spiritual than physical could ever clasp

Marriage is only as strong and legit as two souls make it

If it isn't within you sincerely, no piece of bought paper could fake it

Before Moses, there we were within this institution

After this day, there we will be still in constant evolution

Evolving with time and becoming more woven within the fabric of harmony

Harmoniously travelling with peace and serenity

Others shall hear our laughter as they listen to the gentle summer breeze

Basking in the thought of esoteric ecstasy floating as leaves

On this day we profess in front of our family our devotion to one another

Devotion to be being lovable more than just loving the other

You are my friend first, my connecting piece and my wife

I shall be your friend first, your connection and husband for life

I plead to be all that I was created to be for you

I promise to hold firm to my commitment to us and always be true

True to G-d first and therefore being true to us

Factually right as rain and in truth we must trust

In my heart I know that we were united by our souls before the beginning of time

Light years prior to the meeting of man and mind

So with or without being recognized by a state that may or may not see me as a man

I plead my all to you, so righteously here I stand

Let us cultivate this land that we were given and nurture it so that it may grow

Look into my eyes to see my essence for in you I see all that I need to know

You are my elevation and I intend on being your balance

So on this date, I vow to be to you as you are to me

Your friend, confidant, companion, whatever else I need to be.

In Heaven as it is on Earth

Is a statement that's as immaculate as a child's birth

It is to say that the bliss and joy that is to be expected in the next life

Can be as fulfilling and rewarding as becoming man and wife

This is not 1 person staying with another person until 1 does something wrong

It is a beautiful melody with high notes and a few off keys that still make a wonderful song

The disappearance of the singular noun to be replaced with the collective form

Moving at the same pace carrying the same load, equally yoked is our new norm

Life was never designed for either side to live alone

In the beginning this paradise was a kingdom for a King and Queen to sit on the throne

Ruling over all of creation and maintain the proper structure

Tasting of its fruit, the sweet delectable nectar

The pair was completely incomplete in due form as individuals not yet mated

Much like man wasn't man until the breath of Life allowed him to be formulated

Let us now on this day take this vow in the presence of those whom we love

Let us dwell in the image of the beginning creation to have on Earth as it is above.

I Vow

From this day forward I vow to always be the man of your dreams

I shall make it my goal to each day be way more than what it seems

I promise to love you from now until the end of my days

Even then I ask God to grant me one more chance for us to count the ways

I know at times you think that this man can't possibly be true

But I'm here to tell you that it's so very easy when I was made just for you

Time made us who we are so that we would be ready for the right now in life

Delicate preparation was taken when fulfilling the plan of me being your husband and you as my wife

Just think of all the miscalculations we made throughout our years

It wasn't because we deserved pain it was to appreciate joy you must shed some tears

God doesn't make mistakes but unfortunately sometimes people do

I know that this was no mistake because it was God that sent me you

Each day and night I pray that you are protected and I give thanks for you being in my life

On this day, our day I accept you to forever be my best friend, lover and comforting wife

I know the road will not be perfect but please believe I'll try my best to make it so

To put it plainly I vow to you my life and a love that shall continue to grow.

I Say Yes

Today as I look into your beautiful brown eyes

I thank The G-d above for allowing this to over conceptualize

Take me as I am my dear as I am now so taking you

Bossy, stubborn, and stuck in your ways

Loving, compassionate and 360 wise

Yes

If I must say so myself, and I do say so, you're welcome for such a good selection

Thank you for allowing me to the opportunity to embrace loves perfection

The union of two complete incomplete soul finding one another

Is as momentous as the big bang theory or birth from mother

Yes

No coincidence, no accident just chance in time of chance

In all due time chance and divine planning led to the supposed happenstance

Seven is said to be completion, so seven shall be more completed than more of less

Less fortunate than the levels of heaven that we progress

The seven Wonders of the world, yet there's no wonder why this is and came to be

Seven now and seventy thousand later there will be you and me

Yes

I say yes to forever and never to what was once to know

Me and my mirrored image, as so above so is below.

Anniversary

It's a beautiful morning as the dawn begins to break

The night has passed over and twilight had its mate

The sun is attempting to kiss the sky

Song birds awaken and prepare to fly

Honey dew is calling to be eaten when the reapers take to the field

Nocturnal survivors retire as sleep no longer takes yield

Glory to all that is and how this day is coming to be

Many moons have come and gone so that a new day can we see

Wake up and touch the sky, wake up to a new beginning

Sleep and slumber is over and to lay again is still a sign of winning

Night will follow the day and hopefully being optimistic for the day to again follow the night

Long conversations of searching for answers to questions on what's right

Embracing the new that is to come from the quests that looked to not end

Ending with rain falling upon our face washing away the pollution from within

The dawn has broken and the sun is now shining at will

Pride down, hope up, speak up, face down...peace... be still

Productivity is upon us and rest has come and gone

The night has its purpose so the day must now stand alone

Plurality of the duality yet singularly coming of age

Redefining the day in and day out book with each added page.

Appreciation

Either you appreciate me or you don't

If you want me to love you, I will, otherwise I won't

Either accept me as I am today and how I will be tomorrow

Or let me be as I will be on yesterday and let's just part without any sorrow

No hard feelings for you being you, me being me and us leaving it as it is

I can't fault you not one bit for anything for it ain't what it ain't and it is what it is

It ain't this if it will only be that and it is that since it can't be this

So after all is said and done I guess it can just be known as another day of practice

Another attempt at it so another time at bat to try to at least get on base

Perhaps another chance to study this mystery and label it as a special case

I'm not sure as to how it will all transpire and how the next chapter will read

But what I do know to be a fact is that in life, everyone deserves all or most of what they need

No one should be denied simple pleasures in life and no one should feel less than adequate

Right is right and fair is fair, it is just that simple isn't it?

Away We Go

From boy to man

From can't to can

No longer loving like a boy but man

As real as real can

Be

For she

Is the prize of nobility?

Beauty of fertility

Loving me is a wonder

Yet loving her isn't a moment ponder

Easy

Summer breezy

Lighting the path to heaven on earth

Smiling at sadness so bliss can give birth

Taking my hand to stroll along the golden path

Kissed by God almighty, blessed in His magnificent bath

Rain down on me

The Lord has delivered we

So much time has passed

Yet this prophesy was indeed forecast

Muchas gracias Dios mío

Let us begin to fly, away we go.

<u>Be</u>

It doesn't have to be any more difficult than to just let it be

We are both human and destined for more than the human can see

Being that as it may we are sometimes limited in the vision planned for we

Becoming more of an unit on so many levels that at times they see you in me

Besides the fact that I see me in you and we are more than just two lovers K-I-S-S-I-N-G

Beneath the surface of mere friends we could possibly be

Beknownst, un that is, to me is a sort of melancholy dwelling and waiting to transform

Bench marked by time and ideas of something other than the norm

Benevolent it could be or not perhaps of the perspective of sight

Besties or beasties, equivocally that could be mutual opposition

Beyond it all, to be or not to be will still have to be the question.

Breath

She and I, I and she

Them and us, us and them are we

Paint us a picture of what may become

Be-coming more united into a woven one

Be here with me as I be there with you

Two souls connected in time so that each second be-comes a new

How shall it all come to pass; what is this moment come true?

True indeed a time to converse... parlez-vous

Speaking of persons speaking of Cali- I - for and Nia, so rambunctious and adventurous

Tre - mendously above La-zae blazae actions with us

Mixing Ke with we gives us the luck we need

Yet not stopping short of the 9 that's divine indeed

She and I, I and she

Them and us, us and them are we

Breathe in my essence and exhale my life

Each rebirth is the switching of husband and wife

This time it's me and next time it's you

Regardless the outcome it's the same one of two

Yesterday be-came today and today never left

Within the very soul of each shall remain the others breath.

Change Up

Either it's just my imagination or the reality of translation, she doesn't want me to want her

Perhaps, she doesn't know how to let go so that her heart won't defer

Or should I say deter mine from hers

Circumstances have been blooming for many a years

Yet she recounts too often than not those that don't matter

Who cares about the time that the dog ate the mail or the last of the cake batter

The most important thing was that it bit the man that tried to break in

Yet she focuses on the one or two loses and not the complete win

Wars are won from battle victory and battle defeat

No soldier shall ever go unchallenged forever and never have to get some mud on their feet

There are those moments in which each soldier must make the decision to place their life on the line for the advancement of the entire battalion

There isn't any time for individualism or selfish acts only moments for sacrifices for the nation

So fight the good fight so that the entire team can win the war

Let's not now do as we once have done and get that which we have gotten before.

Enjoying Life

If I were to paint a picture of my devotion to you

It would be a tree full of leaves and fruit in grandeur hue

Each leaf represents my love and each fruit is what has been produced

The manifestation of nurturing the soul that's induced

As a leaf falls it still cannot take away from the immense character that is viewed

Even when the fruit is nothing more than what's ensued

As time continues to press forward and the tree becomes bare

There still isn't anything to fret for the fruit landed with care

Each fruit bared seeds and those seeds began to bloom

A new evolution of love for us to begin to consume

This in turn makes our love timeless, so endless shall we be

A continuous continuum of atomic partials are we

Each life giving birth to the next and the next preparing to give birth further

Much like speaking of infinity is telling one from the other

That which was to come can be remembered by yesterday

So as the past meets the present, so must night transcend into the new day

It is the complimentary compliment that loves to be loved and loving the love that is

The endless cycle of life upon life that makes it so easy to enjoy this.

Crazy

Some days it's crazy how she can make me feel like shit

Almost like an attempt at turning me into a certified bitch

The reality of it all is that I am the man and she is the woman

So in turn I hold her in high esteem, never less always greater than

It's crazy

Seeing myself almost to the point of complete insanity

And not the type of silly, jolly laughing

The type that scientists and psychologists study and make cases studying

I'm crazy

Why should I allow myself to get to this fallacy?

So much aggression because of unrequited emotions

Perhaps it would be different if we could only trade positions

Let's see how that predicament would indeed play out

Perhaps I should just man up and kick that bitch out

That's crazy

So much so because there's no bitch in me

Is it wrong to have a deep and genuine concern for someone that you love and care for?

Is it also wrong for someone to act as though it's not a desire and to practically ignore?

Men acting like women and women acting like men; Oprah, Tyler and Steve got us all topsy turvy

Not sure which way is up Richard, I guess from time to time we all get a little stir crazy.

Forever Will

As the day is long and as the night quickly fade

There you and I stand beautifully, brightly shining blinding the darkest shade

In times gone by and as this time stands still

I love you now, I loved you then and yes tomorrow I still will

I stand before you a completed incomplete man without shame or fear to hide

A simple man that only seeks to have you by his side

Take my hand and together let us further begin this journey in time

In and out of existence, beyond conception of the mind

Space will not be a question nor will there be an incomplete notion to conceive

The reality that we shall make is one that seems too good for others to believe

Yet regardless of their inability to possess the ability to fathom the tranquility of our beautifully woven essence

It is not for the blind to see, the deaf to hear not the ignorant to bear witness of the divine presence

In and out of space, time will forever cease to exist because of the time it has stood still

I have loved you then, I love you now and yes my dear tomorrow I forever will.

Have Not

For her to love me is ok as long as I am not first on the list behind herself and a few others

For me to love her is very easy for she's first and second to none other

Not even my beloved mother

Yet this is still an unbelievable gathering

So why am I feeling left alone with the wandering

There's no place like home, there's no place like home

Where exactly that may be I'm not quite sure because I'm left to roam

When in doubt I guess I could do as they do

Yet I descend from Africans and Native Americans so to myself I must remain true

Meaning I'm in tune with my natural side and with that, nature particularly tends to run its course

Peace be still old gentle soul there isn't any more room for remorse

Let us think of the good so that it may overshadow the bad

Such a melancholy of a time it is, yet it's better to not have but to have had.

How Long?

How long shall I have to wait to see that smile?

How long has it been…way longer than a short while?

I still feel your energy pulling me near

Your fragrance still tickles my inner being and your voice lingers in my ear

It's been several days, in fact a few weeks since we last spoke to one another

For me to not be in your presence; is like a child without its mother

I truly enjoyed seeing you daily and I looked forward to conversing with you

So now that I'm over here and you're still there I am missing my morning to do

I even gave you my number in hopes that you would give a little thought to thinking of me

When you come through those doors each day am I whom you hope to see

So I now I am reminiscing Brian and seeking to borrow a line

"Do I ever cross your mind… anytime?"

I once told you that I would give you a gift from this old heart of mine

Well in fact I am giving you a lot in each line of this rhyme

Without any secret reason or hidden agenda of any kind

This I have designed just for you, the lady in my mind.

Life plus 20

If love is the answer then the question will always be you

This is how am I to decipher between that which was false from what has been proven true

Time in and time out of sync timing has been

Since the days of our youth to the youth of our age once more again

Factual commentary on arbitrary ideas of life and commonalities

Bringing rambunctious innuendoes of memories and déjà vu like practicalities

A story of a love affair for 20 years between me and my friend

So in summation, this is the real song that shall never end

La de da de da daaaa, la de dad de deee

Please pardon me and my moment of feeling so old school Isley

For 20 years I've come to know you and the person that which you are

Yet it has taken me this lifetime of a moment to make it this far

Today is the day that I have long dreamed of and prayed for

Which means that I've also asked for another lifetime to go with this 20 times more.

Lose Control

For me to do tomorrow that which I desire to do today

Makes as much sense as a hungry man putting a steak on layaway

I know what I want and I know how I feel

Being in control may be enjoyable but for now let's just keep it real

There are things in life that are beyond our grasp

This is a reality yet the meaning you still may ask

Some situations are designed to move quickly and some are moderately slow

Some things are a given and some take time to know

At times there may be moments of clarity and others of doubt

Some moments last forever while others you must live without

We could pretend that our entire life we have the blueprint embedded within our very soul

Yet beyond our deepest desire, we still lack complete control

Why try to dictate order to an idea when it isn't within your very own mind

What sense does that really make when you only just waste precious time

That which God has created, He has given a divine purpose and precise instruction

His order precedes chaos, so the beginning was written along with the conclusion

This is to say that sometimes in order to gain the upper hand one must stop wondering why and just let the good times roll

So needless to say, in order to really win it all we must be willing to let loose and lose control.

Loving to Live

Loving to live and alive with this love is what some may call it

A life with love over shadowed with a forecast of living it's said to commit

It said it? It When and how was it said?

When the rose pedals fell and the birds were wed

Seven days a week it must bloom so that the blossom can be fulfilled

No time for breaks or rain checks when kisses must be sealed

Locked and loaded with love so let the shrapnel lie dormant within

From yesterday's shots and tomorrow's life to begin

Ready, aim and fire! No blood in this battle to be loss

Just battle in blood that flows from rivers and boats being toss

High tides and bringing back the Titanic with sweet songs of life

Laughing at the notion that there could ever be lasting strife

Sweet kisses of love that flows with the laughter of life from lips sealed in a kiss

Roses pedals falling noting days to be a miss

Loving life and life of love within walls that isolate the birds of wed

Yesterday's song becomes tomorrow's words that continue to be said.

Moment in Time

If I had to pick any moment in time to capture,

It would be the moment I spend with you

If there was ever a question as to my final answer,

I would have to testify as to that response being completely true

So what makes me certain as to the validity of my thought?

Unequivocally I must confess

In each moment of time I have been given,

Every moment with you truly ranks as one of the best

Before time began and after it comes to close,

Prior to any actual form there we were and this God knows

Two spirits descending from one as a pair,

Given strict instructions on when to meet here back there

A time in time of preparation and formulation

Not as general as 88 for it was an unknown constellation

Twinkle, twinkle little star for 34 years I wondered where thou are

A secret hiding quite near yet appearing so far

Let us unite as we were created before, before time

Me into you and you once again being all mine.

Rainbow

Now I lay me down to sleep

I pray that I never cause her to weep

If either one of us should die before we wake

I shall thank the Lord for the life of love that He did make

My heart has been laid forth for her to have and hold

The afflatus of her and her very being has been a great dream

Sleeping in slumber of time and resting in serene

So softly and gently she looks at me

Saying how and why she loves me as if it couldn't be

Reality...

Seriously...

Vivacious. ..

Salacious...

Dare I give in to her cunning intellect

Will I be a victim or shall I bask in kismet

Look but don't touch, touch but don't look

Kiss and don't tell, keep what you took

Come and do follow, take my hand and let's go

Laying claim to that pot of gold at the end of the rainbow.

Rainbows

Such fluorescent layers of colors are laid

The delicate motion of translucent transition is made

Red, green, yellow, purple and blue

Stop, go, slow down, not changing confusing who

You-

Nor I, yes I step into a realm that's like Alice in Wonderland

Being guided by blind faith that peaks between the fingers in her hand

Stepping in the name of love, dance in the name of what

The name of love of course is how we groove to the melody of us

Watching butterflies flying by

Looking down upon them for they could never be as high

As you and I-

Yet still I try....

Let us fly higher than what could be known

Making our own rainbows from the path we roam

Those that follow will search for the pot of gold

Of you and I, I and you, the greatest love story ever told.

RD

Birthdays are days of birthing future hopefuls and shadows of the projected self

Watching the manifestation of the unconscious build on aging wealth

The fruit of the tree from the roots that dwell within the soil

Earth's bellows nurturing the harvesting of righteousness soul

Feast off of the nectar of life from the loins that proceeded forth

Marching in unison to the beat of all that imaginable worth

Ripened by the sun and time that calculated the exact moment of sweetness

Libations of liberal liberation living for future liveliness

Ahhh... Do you see the past in the seeds of the fruit for the future?

The outer protective layer of stubbornness to neglect an infecting puncture

No worms in this fruit may reside; no flies to call this their home

Just these seeds and the vine to hold tight to for nature to house this home

Let us free, let thee see, let the fruit be good from the tree in which it came

The day of birth being given to it each spring, so Returning Delicious is its name.

Shallow Words

Shallow words that reverberate off an empty wall

Spoken to deafening ears that won't speak at all

What's the issue with those lines and words without meaning?

Never spoken back unless they come far-fetched seeming

Internalized they continue to bounce back and forth around and around the soul they turn

Tell me nothing more than nothing given to the mind unlearn

He told such and such something that such and such told him once before

Nothing more than the soul can spill unto the soulless floor

One of these days the soul will speak out to you and then you will have to hear the sound

Spoken to you while being spoken to when no one is around

Quiet the reverberation that continues to grow and move

Resonating waves given a voice stuttering to be smooth

What's the point, what's the reason for the endless babble that never goes anywhere?

Talking to the man in the mirror for there isn't anyone else to hear.

Sit and Wonder

Why must I sit and wonder as what is to come

Day in and day out I sit and wonder of where I come from

I think on future time and where I shall be

How, when, and why the path I travel shall take me

Walk steadily and persistent on my journey to a time unbeknown

Deep contemplation of past mistakes and hopes becoming fully grown

I wonder where shall I be in life and at point will it all make sense

Sometimes I still feel like that 10 year old climbing that 8ft fence

They say life's a B so death must be a Saint

Because all I Hear now is couldn't and wouldn't, so upon my death I shouldn't hear can't

All this negativity that's being poison to my very being

Move over clouds for my ray of sunshine, because seeing is believing.

Symbol

If I had to give you a symbol of my devotion it would be a sweet kiss

It's soft, warm and innocent yet solidifies a legitimate bliss

Sometimes I think of holding it within the confines of a hug instead

It has the ability to create warmth or compassion never wasted

Yet I could attempt to place it within a spherical metallic that glitters in the morn

Displaying numerical vegetation upon your physique it adorn

A gaze from the eyes could see how it could stare deep into the soul of you

Look within to see without that one without the other one is just a lonely two

A touch of the hand of protection to firmly hold to all that you are

To have it embrace such a delicate flower blooming in a stain glass jar

Shall I speak to you the words that have been embedded upon my heart?

Simple sweet nothings that resonate the renaissance from an equal counterpart

Such extreme measures like ripping out my heart and placing it directly in your hands

This too is a symbol but still not even the wisest could comprehend

So tell me my love, tell me right here and right now

Which of these symbols shall it be, or perhaps just my simple vow

A vow a fidelity to you and all that you are

A vow to us, our future and our destiny upon this star

Thinking/ Reminisce

Each day that I see your smile I become engulfed in bliss

I think of your lovely skin and I think of how we kiss

You have a control over my heart that the laws of medicine cannot explain

I feel that you and I were no only meant to be but are very much the same

Sometimes I wonder if you can ever understand how much I sincerely love and care for you

Perhaps one day this thought will only be a memory of what was untrue

She loves me, she loves me not, she loves me, she loves me...never not

There is only she loves me just as there is only a Sun that is hot

Why do I love her so, so why should I not love her at all

Why must the world revolve around the sun, why must leaves turn brown and fall?

Why must there be a why, why can't it all just be

Perhaps we should just keep on living so that in time
we can reminisce and see.

This Becomes That

I wished upon a star for a love of my own

To grow old with a love and not just to grow old and grown

There is a very big difference in being happy and living in happiness

Much like being fine and not having finesse

So what would make one so content with being unfulfilled?

Much in the sense of buying containers never sealed

Rolling the dice on a chance that chance will be kind when it isn't the norm

Taking a moment to taste the rainbow in the midst of a hail storm

Hurt-

Why...

Not I, not you

Where's the happily ever after that's spoken of in the stories?

The sweet dream that I've seen in the romantic movies

That's what we all want... isn't it?

Not this sink hole of hope and falling into a never ending pit

Disparity-

This can't be life, I refuse to accept it as such

That dream of bliss is heaven and it's said not to cost much

Deny myself...not happiness just unhappiness being content with not

Not being loved or loveable

Which in sense is being alive without living or livable

With or without a purpose, is this what life is all about

I can't believe that... I refuse to accept this life without

The order is the husband adorns the wife and Allah is to adorn him like a hat

So why should I accept this...when I've been promised that.

Tonight

Tonight as I lay myself down to sleep

I think of you and I fight not to weep

I reminisce of the days that have past

And I wish for another chance to make them last

When I say that I miss you, you need to know that I mean it

How we conversed and reciprocated one another's wit

Let me just lay here and dream of you and I

Let me awaken to this dream and not to a disappointing sigh

Touch the Sky

To say that you and I are together in this life is more of an understatement than birth means life

For one day I shall take you in my arms to have and to hold well beyond a typical husband does a wife

So how shall I have you and more so how shall you be held?

What description shall be given to two souls bonded stronger than the most industrious weld

Taking flight throughout time and on the 7th level of heaven

Blessed in each life time beyond measure of true progression

In love, of love, before love and with it

Have me, hold me and embrace me; meshed to a perfect fit

Hear my thoughts from the other side of the earth

Share my sorrow within and outwardly with my mirth

Let me bask upon your smile and gaze upon your desire

Let us taste the sweet nectar of love that is to transpire

Look within my very being and see that which is meaningful

Show me your being and give praise for Him being so merciful

Beneficent

Most intimate

Translucently translucent

Exceptionally proficient

Limited by reality yet unlimited by what's imaginable

For what's within to touch the sky is left to be unfathomable.

Transitional Moments

Sitting here watching the sun as it peeks over the horizon

Listening to the night as it whispers and whimpers of the inevitable end

The glorious morning light it is indeed

Silence those tears young one and witness a magnificent deed

Truth is in that act so it must manifest the birth of change

Changing from darkness so in light I'm in

Scattering thoughts of wonderment...

Confusion...

Delusion...

What's next could be construed as intrusion

Enter courses, so into me you see

Woe is man and man is at a loss with or without she

Man speak life into them dry bones and peacefully understand each piece

Each piece of my peace is amiss when compare and contrast cease and desist

The reflection of man must look at the image to see they are both the same

Differently positioned yet the same pieces within the game

Truth

Whisper to me something that will give life to the dead

They can't both exist in this realm yet they are transitional moments to wed.

Wait

Patience isn't just a word that many aren't familiar with, it's also a noun that must be developed. Developed into a mountainous strength from the bellows within, deep down within the soul. Frank Swinnerton says it is like, "Waiting patiently, in silence, as a cat does at a mouse hole." Must I sit by and slowly move my tail as I wait for her to come out of her titanium shell that seems to crack and heal, crack and heal.....waiting and wanting her to come on out so I may have what I desire... or must I think of it as Sharon Olds put it," Patient, like an old man who has just dug his grave." One day it shall come but when.... how long must I wait??? Am I seeking to rush into a horrible fate or is it a sweet conclusion to a delightful story?? On the one hand I could be waiting on something that will never come as she has retreated out the back exit or perhaps I'll just wait myself to death and unto death I shall reside. Patience is a noun not a verb, it doesn't require any action, just time and space. Time to be and space to exist for a moment of time that isn't determined until it's over and space that isn't measured until it's been viewed. So I wait, continue to wait and wait and wait and wait some more...wait until to tide no longer sees the shore. Wait until the sun has burned up the moon. Wait until the Universe sends the Earth into an Old Blue Eyes swoon. Wait and wait on young man until the age of time has taken ahold of your bones and the fight within your soul. Wait until waiting is no longer the goal.

Circles

Does she see me as I see me?

Or does she see me as she see me?

Do I see her as I see her?

Or do I see here as she sees her?

Is it the image in the mirror that she sees when see me?

Or perhaps the image that lies behind the veil of imagery?

Will I see her as she should be viewed?

Or am I witnessing a mirage, is my vision obscured?

Does the sun twinkle still when I look into her eyes?

Am I still the adoration she possessed, am I the dream in disguise?

Will I be the last breath that she takes as she gasps for more?

Could she be wings that lift this weakened body off the floor?

Should I kiss her with a forbidden passion as if it was taboo?

Could she think of me with heat flames roaring as volcanos do?

Is there a moment that she needs that I seem to have forgotten?

I wonder if I hold her attention without it being woefully gotten

Are we just two souls racing thru time?

Or are we two old souls wandering with lost minds?

Wandering aimlessly in a circle, smiling yet wandering how did we get here

Not caring too much as we kiss and pull each other near.

Take One

The scene is set and the lights are programmed to glow

A faint light illuminates the room and the director starts the show

The audience is patiently waiting for the actors to begin their lines

This is a live performance, so there isn't a chance to rewind

Poised and positioned for a once in a lifetime portrayal of a modern day love scene

No time for an extra rehearsal, this shot must be tight and clean

If a fumble is made and line has been forgotten

Adlib the next line until your former position as been gotten

Just remember what you came for and what it is that you initially sought

Never lose focus of the end game as well as the beginning since it's the middle that's the longest

The extras are here to distract you, so your game has to be the strongest

Stay focused

The stage is lit and the scene is set

It is time to begin, the cast has met

Everyone take you positions and prepare for action

Actor looks at the actress and she looks at him

The curtain rolls up, director tells action, she and him becomes them.

Penny For Your Thoughts

Sometimes you just have to say, oh what the hell

Throw your hands up and pitch that penny into the wishing well

Wishing for a piece of a glimpse that the filed will begin to be leveled

As magnificent as the horizon appears over the open field un-meddled

Perhaps a penny won't do and a nickel or a dime is needed instead

I could use every ounce of these coins to help me to get somewhat ahead

Throw it into the abyss and watch it as it slowly disappears into the unknown

I see it, I see it I no longer can witness it and to where it has gone

Has the sun tilted and has it not stayed flat upon the square

Does the penny for my thoughts fall into the well I don't care

Would someone please hand me a quarter or a Bo dollar as I need more to deposit for relief

It's beginning to feel like a very long distance call with no understanding, capisce?

Do you speak English or am I wishing in a foreign well?

Is there someone down there snatching my wish along with each coin? I can't tell

I've thrown about a buck fifty already and my pockets aren't jingling as they once were

Is this the point where I just accept what is and no longer seek to deter?

Or is it vice versa and perhaps my wish came after some other?

Am I too late to come up for air; must I be conquered and smothered

Wait, I believe I can see it a little clear now the bubble floating helped to make it all true

I'm the coin being tossed in the well and the wisher was you

This means I'm falling to the bottom and losing sight of from whence I came

Drowning in the thoughts of what is and isn't of the lights out game

Pennies, nickels, dimes and a quarter

Bo dollars, no dollars, hopeless wishes with no order

The sun has finally set; the possibility of witnessing the horizon has faded with it

Yet a flicker of light from the moon brings new hope with it.

www.ingramcontent.com/pod-product-compliance
Lightning Source LLC
Chambersburg PA
CBHW031421040426
42444CB00005B/665